Under The Crumbling Stars

by

Vicki Mickelson

the Peppertree Press
Sarasota, Florida

Dedication

For Craig,

with whom I share the memories.

Acknowledgements

Love and thanks to Jerry for supporting my annual three-month exit.

A special thanks to Liberty and Aanya for embracing their grandmother with love, compassion, and acceptance.

A big hug and thanks to Aunt Voni who will always be Mom's embracing, affectionate, and encouraging little sister.

Many thanks to members of AAUW Writers Group and Gulf Coast Writers Guild for intently listening to my work and offering constructive suggestions and support.

Also, a huge thank-you to Julie Ann James of Peppertree Press for lighting the fire.

And a heartfelt thanks to Debbie and Bill Kilichowski who provide my winter writing sanctuary.

Contents

Framed Perfection

*

When visitors arrived
I sat in the corner
All blue eyes and flannel warmth
Clutching my furry pink pajama doll
I didn't have to speak
I was the quiet child
No match for Mom's obsessive verbalry
Zipping and unzipping the closed-eyed doll's back
Wishing I could crawl into her spine
And remain
Wrapped in framed flannel forever

Manic Mama

*

I don't ever remember having a bedtime
Nights were a magical veil
Filled with midnight shopping trips to Holiday
And impromptu baking sessions
The upstairs eves sprouted
Enormous plates of cut out sugar cookies and fudge

I never asked why

I just knew the darkness produced
Frenetic energy that prompted chain smoking
And unexplained verbal motion
Sometimes shouting and chasing me
With a vacuum cleaner hose
Flicking it at my butt
As I flew up the slippery nylon carpeted stairs
To safety behind a locked bathroom door
Hours later, a pounding
As I sat sobbing on the toilet cover
Staring out the window at the constellations
An apology
And then more darkness
As she plunged into days of demon-like sleep
I
Gaining my freedom
Never asking why

Needing Swan Lake

*

At age 3 ½ I tied my ice skates together
Flung them around my neck
Over my wrinkly red snowsuit
And wobbled nine blocks
To the neighborhood skating rink

Alone

My brother was a newborn
A high-pitched screamer
A puker

Mom couldn't smoke enough Pall Malls
To quell the lack of sleep
In her hollow mind cave

No more quiet corner for me

Strangers helped me lace up
I forged ahead then fell
In rhythm to "Swan Lake"
Waltzing in circles
Shadowing lopsided figure 8's
Ungraceful

Filling my own hollow cave
With shaved ice
To ¾ time

Alone

Under the crumbling stars

Carrie's Ghost

*

Every mild-weathered day
When I'd rather be building forts or rollerskating
Mom plopped my brother in the buggy
Yelled, Let's go
And we trekked a mile and a half
To Great-Grandma Nelson's
I didn't fuss
Trimming the apple tree
Pruning bushes and
Dusting the snake plants
In the sun-spotted dining room
Were taken for granted
A snarl on Gram's Swedish profile
As she rolled out flat bread
A pound chunk of soft butter awaiting slathering
Greeted us past the upright piano
Baby, her beloved green parakeet
Landed on my shoulder
Plucked dots from my yellow dotted Swiss dress
The same dress I always wore to visit

One day there was no flat bread aroma
Baby rambled on in Swedish while plucking
Leaving my shoulder barren

I was left with dusty plants and a baby buggy
While Mom found Grams
Still in her bed, still
With chest-heaving sobs
Producing no tears
Shrieks muffled by layers of wallpaper
She wept for the woman who raised her
The stubborn lady who left coal in her Christmas stocking

Floundering Fishy

On the bottom of a black wooden trunk
Folded between yellowed tissue paper pieces
My first dance costume breathes

Mom pieced together the gold lame'
Hand sewed strategically placed metallic green fins
On a bubble butted 4-year-old's two piece
Including a boat-shaped hat

I'm sure she was proud of me
But she never said

I sang "Three Little Fishies in a Fish Pond"
And tapped my black patents in a shuffle step
But she never said

I was center stage
Red rosebud lips
Blond curls like Shirley Temple
Shiny fins
Gold lame'

But she never said

Absent Mom

*

My dress, blue brocade
The bow perfectly tied
Rested its sash
At the peak of my crack
Relaxed
Not like me
Cherubic 5-year-old cheeks
Crimson face muscles
Thumping
Thumping
Trying to smile
Solitaire soul
Mirrored in strapped Mary Janes
Encasing scrunched lace-edged Buster Brown anklets
Disguising the dread
Of being the only kindergartner
Without her mom on Day 1
Not the lure of the sandbox
The upright piano
Stationed at an angle awaiting song
Nor
The fully equipped playhouse
Uprooted my hanging head
Until the floor puddle beneath Timmy widened
In front of me

Threatening my reflection
His tears immersing themselves
As dripping snot
On my upper lip
And I licked them away
Over and over and over
To the ting of the metal triangle

Break Time

*

Walking home for lunch
Was mandatory in elementary school
But one day I had Campbell's vegetable soup
At the yellow house across the street

Everyone else went home to Mom and Casey Jones
My mom was on a break
The doctor told her to get a job
Stresses from having a second child
A sick child
An energetic child
Had exhausted her

While my classmates returned to school
Singing Casey's birthday song
I fought back a black fear
That one day
I may need a break also
And there would be
No birthday song for me

Cake in the Oven
Candy in the Dish

*

There was never a day orange slices, spearmint leaves or
party mints
Weren't heaped in the milk glass candy dish
Always 'candy from Sandy', Mom's nickname
And usually a devils food cake
In an aluminum rectangular pan
Placed in the oven for snacks
I indulged

Mom acquired a prescription for Preludin
An amphetamine
For me when I was seven
Three times a day
Six days a week I swallowed the square pink pills
Sunday was my "free" day

The pounds disappeared
I was in the spotlight
No longer wearing hand-me-downs from my cousin
Mom purchased a black and white print dress
With rick rack trim

The same one Angela Cartwright wore
On "The Danny Thomas Show"
And I was
Then worthy of a photo
On the front step

B is for Brownies

*

Talking, chatting
Chatty, talky, talky, chatty
Mouth rumbling, an art
Evenings
PTA secretary
E-E-E-E is for Education
Chatty Sandy
Sunday
K-K-K-K is for kitchen serving
D/C donuts and coffee
So much to do
So much to say
Talk, chat
Promises to shop at Southdale
P-P-P-P is for promises
Oops! No can do
Maybe a picnic in the park
Sounds great
Oops! Gotta run and pick up festival prizes
E is for Education
But guess what?
I'm your new Brownie leader
We'll wear brown uniforms

Make sit upons
Cook a boiled dinner over a bonfire
Sing songs while roasting marshmallows
S-S-S-S is for Singing
All with a troop of eleven
Chat
Talk
B-B-B-B-is for Brownies
And
Broken promises

Never Pretty in Pink

*

Sporting a short boy-styled haircut
And much anticipation
I hopped the 19B to go downtown
My favorite place
Dayton's, Donaldson's, Power's
Never disappointed
Nine years, by myself
I chose a pair of pink shorts
And a blocked pastel pink and blue top
At Dayton's 4th floor without hesitating
I rarely wore pink
Envying the cotton candy poodle skirts and angora sweaters
Other girls adorned
Mom was olive skinned
With brown hair and eyes
She smothered my fair complexion in unflattering warm tones
I knew she would disapprove
But I purchased the outfit anyway
Longing for Pepto pink to drape my skin
I modeled the soft cotton duo
Dad squinted above his glasses and smiled
Mom clutched the gray Dayton's bag with red lettering
Plotting a return
And again
I was
Never pretty in pink

Beaver Syndrome

*

I thought my family was "Leave it to Beaver"
Until I realized Mom didn't wear
Fitted dresses with cute collars
And high heels around the house
And when her voice bellowed
In a wave of rage
Scaring my brother out of the house
Butterfly net in hand
And me riveting
Hopping on my blue Schwinn
To pedal around Lake Nokomis
Stopping only to check my wire handlebar basket
For an apple
I knew June Cleaver
Would never allow
Her voice to be raised in such fury
Like black grime smothering a pug nose
Instantly lining the nostrils with soot
Choking the mass upward
Then down the throat
Gravel in the esophagus
Tainting the apple's sweetness

Plucking for Pennies

*

Every fourth month
My parents hosted a neighborhood card club
Four couples seated around the kitchen table
Four TV trays
One at each corner
Filled with mixed nuts
And Fanny Farmer chocolates
A bevy of liquor lined the counter
A filled-to-the-brim ice bucket
Highball glasses at the ready
It was the only time Mom cleaned the house
Piles of newspapers disappeared
The Hoover canister got a workout
Empty soup cans disposed of
Pans scrubbed and put away
Ajax bleached the white porcelain sink
My brother and I holed up in the living room
TV, 16 ounce RC colas, bowls of pretzels our companions

The morning after
We plucked for pennies under the table
Adding them to our piggy banks
My escape money
The kitchen no longer so clean
I knew the dirty dishes, open cans of nuts

Uncapped liquor bottles, and candy-strewn floor
Bore my name
With not enough pennies
And no one else to shake the cleanser can
My escape was delayed
Once again

Road Trip

*

A shimmery 1963 Chevy station wagon
Two kids, two pillows
Suitcases haphazardly strapped on the top luggage carrier
Bags of midget tootsie rolls and Kraft fudgies
One AAA trip tik
And many desolate hours ahead
Destination: Florida
Daydreaming scenarios about Johnny Crawford and Paul
Petersen
Acting behind a velvet curtain
Avoiding the front seat massacre of words
Playing alphabet word games
Until dusk
Mangy motel
Mom's verbal tirades
Exhausting
Bellowing snores
Not silenced by the uneven chop
Of the window air conditioner
The bathtub becomes my boat
The pillow my sound barrier mast
Maybe I'll be caressed by a dripping faucet wave
Transported once again behind the velvet curtain

Where I wrap my arms around Paul and Johnny
And travel my own road trip
Playing alphabet word games
With the road kill

Rockwell Holidays

*

At Christmas and every other holiday
Theme became an obsession
In a good way sometimes
Lists and lists of planning
Days and days of shopping
And all night preparation
No sleep
Nothing accomplished good enough
The bone-in rump roast in the basement oven
The 25# turkey sizzling in the kitchen
Ping pong table decorated and set for twenty-two
Two adorned Christmas trees
Rice pudding equipped with a hidden almond
Three-foot diameter trays laden with Spritz, wedding
balls, sugar cookies, rocky road bars and fudge

The stage set
The players ready
Mr. Rockwell would be proud
Break a leg!

A good time was had by all

Wait for the flash
Click ... and ... Crash
The tree topper stars crumble
Into tiny glass fragments
To be swept up by me
And tediously glued together for next year's photo

Period Monger

*

In seventh grade
I rushed home from school
With the most amazing news
Finally
Mom was supervising Indian Guides
With my brother's tribe
In the basement
Signaling and shouting
I got her attention
Softly and proudly I explained my period had arrived
I expected her to run upstairs
Enfold me in her arms
And celebrate
Instead
She hollered, "The curse?
You know where the pads are."
My secret now fodder
For the 10-year-old boys in feather headbands
Blood dripping slowly
A sacrifice to the guide mother
Who didn't practice the guidelines

Silence Not So Golden

*

After a verbal Mom episode
I was the non-mediator
The go-between
When my parents didn't speak
The silence unrelenting
Lasted days
And sometimes days longer
808 square feet of bungalow
Squished into a 6'x6' space
Around the kitchen table
Mashed potatoes slapped on plates
One pork chop each
Cottage cheese with a half canned peach for Dad
And silence
Until Mom blurts, "Tell your father . . ."

More silence

Again, "Tell your father . . ."
Heaving a fork on her empty plate
She retreats in a heated huff
Dad, eating his peach in methodical quiet
Me, gaping in disbelief
Always caught unaware
With mashed potatoes seething between my teeth
Lumping behind mercury-filled molars
In not-so-golden silence

Sunday Morning Angel

✳

"Is that what you're wearing to church?"
"Yes."
It's too short."
"I like the flow of the skirt."
"Go upstairs and change, now!"
"Don't scream."
"You're telling ME what to do?"

I no longer feel
The flare of designer purple
Hugging my hips in royal victory
The designer skirt has become
A thrift store
Moth-eaten
Misshapen
Piece of wool
I refuse to recognize

Trudging up the brown tweed staircase
Crystals falling from my shattered tiara
By a slice of truncated wicked
My halo tumbling
I am no longer
The
Sunday morning angel

Sno Ball

*

In February 1967
I attended my high school
Winter formal dance
With Jim, my suburban boyfriend
Mom was all excited and splurged
Gown from Dayton's
Pea green crepe, umpire waist
With a bow centered between my boobs
Short puffy sleeves
Long white gloves
White ballet slippers
Hair piece of real hair for an up-do
purchased from
Gretchen, her stylist
Lorraine sewed a white mohair
Floor-length coat
My curfew was extended to 4:00 am
Since the after party was at my dance studio
And chaperoned
Regal
I was Grace Kelly descending the snow-covered steps

But there was no carriage
Another girl had my exact dress
Jim never told his mom he would be staying out until 4
Fruit punch didn't set the mood
And pea green wasn't my color
I still have the picture somewhere of my sallow skin
In dim lighting with no smile

Lorraine bragged for months
She had picked
the perfect dress

At 17 . . .

*

My hair turned dishwater blond
Mousy, lackluster
I hadn't noticed much
But Mom wasn't ready
To give up the childhood sunshine

She bought a bleach kit
A plastic cap with holes
Like mouse droppings
And a crochet hook
Sat me down under a plastic table cloth
And turned me into a streak freak

How could I let her down?

Revlon Blond Silk became my monthly companion
Natural locks transformed
Into overall Marilyn platinum
Stripping every strand to anorexia
Until one day I brushed too hard
And the fragile crisp clumps tumbled
Shadowing white porcelain

A loss of childhood
Swirling down the drain
In effigy to sunny innocence

Mother Friend

*

As a teenager
I envisioned all moms
Acting as their daughters' best friends
Like Lorraine did with me
Hiding upstairs
Hunkered down on the sewing room floor
As Ed sauntered to the front door
After hip jumping
Out of his new top-down convertible
A gift from Uncle Sam
After a frontline stint in Viet Nam
She
Creepily lifting her head
To view his scrubbed face
He
Squinting angrily
After fist beating the doorbell
Knowing he was stood up
Foot stomping the sidewalk in stupidity
She
Exclaiming
"Mission accomplished!"

Pageant Princess

*

Cinderella
Pure, good, innocent, worthy
A princess at her own ball

Me
Miss Teen South Minneapolis finalist
In a $10 sale gown
Tall, thin, confident, in control
Smiles
No fumbles
Never any fumbles
Honest answers
Eye contact
Applause, applause
And yet . . .
First runner-up
The glass slipper, now acrylic
Didn't quite fit

"They had to give it to the black girl,"
Mom said with seething eyes

No fairy dust
No ball
No hug

Midnight darkness came early

Travel On . . .

*

Senior year
David was the love of my life
A year older, he attended college
Smoked pot
Played chess in cubbyholes on Cedar Riverside
Was a poet
A guitar player
And a cheapskate
Who couldn't spell
I adored his black-rimmed glasses
His soap-scented skin
His dream of building a log home
In the western woods for us to live off the land
His love of Simon and Garfunkel
His belief in faith healing

My mother wasn't fond of him
Each night he picked me up
In his blue winged-fin '59 Chevy
She sent a travel alarm
Set to 12:45 AM
Knowing we'd park
Around Lake Nokomis
For a late night make-out session
Steaming the windows

Droplets of moisture cascading
To the rhythm of our exhales
Black-rimmed glasses rumbling on the dashboard

One night the travel alarm
Tucked neatly in the glove compartment
Went ignored
The ringing blending silently
With rivulets of split ends
Dancing on plastic seat covers

I arrived home at 1:08 AM
Eight minutes past my curfew
The front door was locked
Outside light extinguished
My packed suitcase was on the step
And Mom's werewolf eyes
Glared outward from the slim window in disdain

I, a recluse in my own yard
Became a black light monster
Surfing the snow-capped Tetons
In a basement bedroom on 29th Avenue
Eight minutes late to the party

The Not-So Escape

*

Ninety minutes of road time distance
I could feel the freedom ooze from my pores
No more structured days
No yelling
No derogatory comments
No slapping vacuum cleaner hoses
Skimming my butt
No curfew
No reason to be perfect
Freedom

College adjustment, an enigma
No more Dad to guide me through algebraic equations
An older dorm roommate
Who borrowed my negligee
For a motel rendezvous
Small town kids
Who taught the city girl how to shop lift
From tiny downtown stores

Home for a weekend
Target the target
Empty purse
Now filled with scarves, belts
Caught

Finger printed
Booked

*

Parents telephoned
No words spoken
I wanted to
No apology, no tears
I wanted to

Court appearance
$25 fine which Dad paid
Thank you
And still
No words spoken

Back to the escape plan
College
Freedom under the salacious stars
Maybe
Holding my tongue
While
Swallowing lightning bolts

Wedding Pains

*

College graduation: June 9th
Wedding date: August 12th
In between I served chicken cordon bleu
To paunchy supper club businessmen
In Mankato
Until Mom called sobbing
She was ill
In pain
And needed surgery

"We'll postpone the wedding"
"You can't do that"
"But you're in pain"
Sobs and more sobs and sighing sobs

A uterine tumor, grapefruit size
Lots of pain
No one aware and in wedding expectation
The purple cake needed a center water fountain
And Norwegian cup cake topper
Flowers for bouquets needed to be picked
From neighbors' gardens
The turkey and wild rice needed her approval
The outdoor ceremony site needed stems and bows

My brother's band plucked and strummed
The Cold Duck, seven cases, flowed
While Mom played Master
Concealing her protruding pain
Beneath a yellow sheath
To
"Whiter Shade of Pale"

Locked In

*

The front door slammed
Dead bolt clicked
There will be no doctor visit
Probable stroke
Possible diabetes
Definite disease of the heart
No doctor visit
Five months of not answering the phone
Calling for pizza and chicken delivery
Bones decaying on the kitchen carpet
Blending stench with rotten bananas
Fruit flies feasting with maggots
And still, no doctor visit
Until Friday night, Urgent Care
She finally succumbs
After fifty years and a locked-in five months
I become the chosen
Hospital
Toe amputation
Leg arteries unclogged
Rehab
Heart attack
Alone in tandem
All of it my fault
Antiseptic mind
Locked in guilt
Shrill screams accompanying my sickly shadow

The Lion Growls

*

"Your mother is a doll
So agreeable and sweet"
The nurses reiterate over and over

The disguise shattered when I enter the hospital room

"Grrrrrr . . . . . ."

She's ready to pounce
The pastel aura lifted
Dragon fire

"Grrrrrr . . . . . ."

Booming blackness
Bouncing off sterile green walls
Brown eyes penetrating my sternum
Reverberating slander

I am once again
The quiet child
Who zips and unzips my pink pajama doll
Seeking spinal refuge under an open sky
Hoping for a sullen sunrise
Before the stars again
Begin to disintegrate
Blown under the covers by the lion's growl

Little Fib

*

"You lied to me"
You finally found out
she spat from her nursing home wheelchair
Heaving the TV remote

Hidden under several stained towels
On the top shelf
Of an upstairs linen closet
A wedding album
September 24, 1949
Not 1948
Mom in a custom-made peplum suit
A slight baby bump
Me, the size of a pea
Amniotic fluid surrounding
Protected, warm, unknowing
For the last time
Tiny silhouetted fragments of fetal tissue
Already crumbling
While
An anonymous guest at her wedding

Eulogy Never Spoken

*

DOD: 10/15/2002

My mother was an artist
Not an artist in the conventional sense
But an artist nonetheless
She painted each day
With a different hue of the rainbow

As a young child
She offered me a red wool blanket
Perfect for throwing over back yard clothes lines
Securing with rocks from the retaining wall
Calling it a tent, my heaven
Pretending I was camping
She completed the gesture with a flashlight
And chocolate chip cookies

One Saturday morning
I got up and made orange juice
From a frozen can of concentrate
Throwing the can in the garbage was a no-no
We were saving them for a neighborhood Hobo Breakfast
Pajamas, orange juice in cans, pancakes & sausage
On tin plates, no utensils
In our back yard
A surprise wake up for the neighbors

Cake decorating became her forte'
After many hours of practice
And disposing of wax paper frosting holders
Mom culminated her skill
With a yellow doll cake
For my 8th birthday
The dark-haired doll beauty
Became the center
Her skirt – layers and layers of yellow icing
Tiny pink rosebuds adorning
My own Sleeping Beauty

Constantly redecorating the house
Mom's creative imagination
Spewed ceremonious results
The living room walls would become green
A deep olive green like no one else's
Never apprehensive about digging in
She painted the walls herself
Accompanying them with matching carpet
An 84" zig-zagged print velvet sofa
And a mesmerizing swan painting above

In elementary school I needed a costume quickly
I was Little Bo Peep in a class play
Without hesitation I was smothered in white pantaloons
A blue "Little House on the Prairie" dress
And bonnet she sewed herself
Time was short

The zipper never appeared
But hidden safety pins secured the fabric
I was the best dressed nursery rhyme
Nothing could hide my smile

When aqua was still the kitchen rage
Mom decided purple would be her accent color
Searching everywhere for linens, spatulas, glassware
Her determination unrelentless
Her vision skimming reality
Purple materialized
From the back corners of TR Christian and Dayton's
Her kitchen emerged complete and stylish
Way ahead of its time

I wanted an indigo wedding gown
Lavender I would settle for
Mom said it wasn't going to happen
I must wear white
We compromised on white eyelet
With holes large enough for the blue-violet underskirt
To show through
The same shade as my bouquet

Red, orange, yellow, green, blue, purple, indigo
The palette of an artist
Not in the conventional sense
A Mom artist
Who showed her love
Through her creative spirit

Thank you, Mom
For showing me the colors of the rainbow
Beyond the stars
I Love You

About the author/poet

*

When Vicki Mickelson was in second grade she wrote a short story titled "It Rained Blue Snow". Her teacher, impressed with her imagination, gave her accolades and insisted she read it to the class. She has been writing ever since.

Thirty-eight years as an educator in middle and high school English classrooms gave Vicki the opportunity to cultivate a love of writing in her students. Since retiring, she now pursues that love herself.

Vicki resides in Minnesota with her husband. She spends winters in Anna Maria, Florida.

CPSIA information can be obtained
at www.ICGtesting.com
Printed in the USA
FFOW03n0028191015
17736FF

9 781614 933588